The Mayo Brothers

Community BUILDERS

Community BUILDERS

The Mayo Brothers

Doctors to the World

by Lucile Davis

Children's Press®
A Division of Grolier Publishing
New York London Hong Kong Sydney
Danbury, Connecticut

Photo Credits

Photographs ©: Corbis-Bettmann: 7; Courtesy of Mayo Clinic Communications: cover, back cover, 2, 9, 12, 14, 15, 19, 21, 22, 23, 24, 26, 27, 28, 31, 32, 33, 34, 35, 37, 39, 40, 42, 43; Minnesota Historical Society: 16; Olan Mills Portrait Studio: 48; Photo Researchers: 8, (SPL), 17 (Will & Deni McIntyre), 44 (Lawrence Midgale); Superstock, Inc.: 45; The StockShop Inc.: 3 (Scott Berner).

Reading Consultant
Linda Cornwell, Learning Resource Consultant
Indiana Department of Education

Visit Children's Press on the Internet at:
http://publishing.grolier.com

Library of Congress Cataloging-in-Publication Data

Davis, Lucile.
    The Mayo brothers : doctors to the world / by Lucile Davis.
        p. cm. — (Community builders)
    Includes bibliographical references and index.
    Summary: A biography of the world-famous doctors who established the Mayo Clinic, funded numerous medical studies, and contributed thousands of dollars to their home city of Rochester, Minnesota.
    ISBN: 0-516-20965-5 (lib. bdg.)   0-516-26347-1 (pbk.)
    1. Mayo, William James, 1861-1939—Juvenile literature. 2. Mayo, Charles Horace, 1865-1939—Juvenile literature. 3. Physicians—Minnesota—Biography. 4. Mayo Clinic—History—Juvenile literature. [1. Mayo, William James, 1861-1939. 2. Mayo, Charles Horace, 1865-1939. 3. Physicians. 4. Mayo Clinic—History.] I. Series.
R154.M33D38 1998
610'.92'2776—DC21
[B]   97-35783
                                                                              CIP
                                                                               AC

Contents

Imagine This

Imagine the year is 1855. You and your family live in a small town on the Western frontier in Minnesota Territory.

One day you get sick with a terrible stomachache. Your mother gives you hot tea, then puts you to bed. After a few days, your stomachache is getting worse. Your father sends for a doctor. When the doctor comes, he feels your forehead. Then he touches the tender spot on your stomach.

The doctor doesn't know much about your illness. In fact, he knows only two things. First, you have an infection in your stomach. (An infection is an illness

6

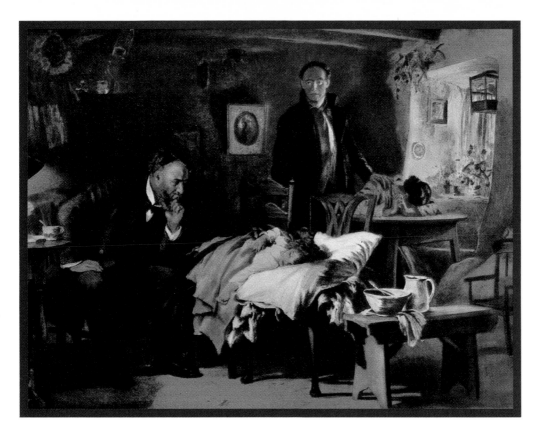

**As anxious parents wait, the doctor
considers the cause of their child's illness.**

that is caused by germs.) Second, many people die
from the infection.

Your parents ask if anything can be done to help
you. The doctor says an operation might help, but he
does not know how to do it. Your parents ask if there
is a place where they can go for help. The doctor
says there is a surgeon at a hospital who can do the
operation. But the hospital is many miles away.

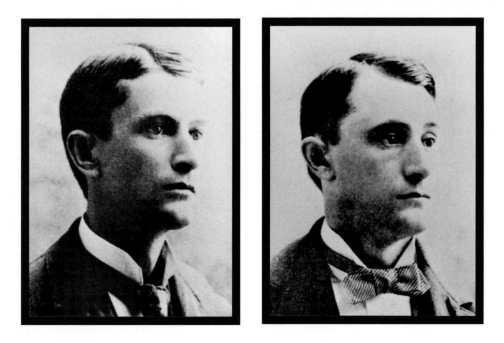

Dr. William Mayo (left) and Dr. Charles Mayo (right)

How lucky you are to be living today. If you had that same kind of stomachache, your doctor would know what to do. He would tell you that you have appendicitis (uh-pen-duh-SYE-tiss). This is an infection of a small tube inside you called your appendix. You would go to a nearby hospital where a doctor would remove your appendix while you are asleep. After the operation, you would feel better. In a few days, you would go home. After a few weeks, you would be able to play with your friends again.

Two brothers named William and Charles Mayo were doctors. Together, they changed the way doctors practice medicine. The Mayos also helped to establish a safe way to operate on people. They became very successful. They built a clinic—a place where patients can go for medical care. People from all over the United States and around the world went to the Mayos for help.

The Mayo brothers gave their own money to make sure the Mayo Clinic could go on without them. Today, the clinic continues to treat patients and to teach doctors from all over the world. This is the story of how William and Charles Mayo became known as "doctors to the world."

This 1996 photograph shows Mayo Clinic, one of the best-known hospitals in the world.

Rochester, Minnesota

Minnesota became a state in 1858. The city of Rochester is located in the southeastern part of the state. Rochester began as a farming community. In 1863, about 1,500 people lived there. Today, Rochester is a major medical center with a population of 77,000 people.

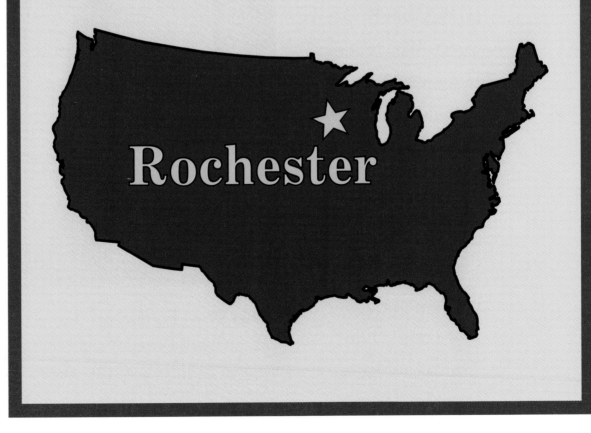

Rochester

Chapter TWO

Doctors in Training

William James (Will) Mayo was born on June 29, 1861, in the village of LeSueur, Minnesota. Three years later, his father, Dr. William Worrall Mayo, moved the family to Rochester. At that time, there were four children in the family—Will, Sarah, Gertrude, and Phoebe. On July 19, 1865, another boy, Charles Horace (Charlie), was born.

As soon as Charlie was able to walk, he and Will were pals. They were always together. One of their favorite things to play with was the kettle full of bones in their father's office. The boys learned how to build a human skeleton. Their father taught them

11

Dr. and Mrs. William Worrall Mayo and their daughters—Sarah, Phoebe, and Gertrude—posed for this photograph during the 1860s.

about each part of the skeleton. This is how they learned anatomy (uh-NAT-uh-mee). Anatomy is the structure of the body of a person or an animal.

The boys' father also taught them about chemistry (KEM-is-tree). Chemistry is the study of what things are made of. Their mother taught them botany (BOT-uh-nee), which is the study of plants. At night, the boys looked through their mother's telescope, and she told them about the stars and the planets.

12

Charlie and Will especially liked helping their father with his medical practice. Sometimes the boys would go with him to see his patients. During these trips, Dr. Mayo would explain to the boys what

Medicine in the 1800s

In the 1800s, there were few hospitals or clinics. The local doctor took care of anyone who was sick or injured. Most doctors' offices were in their homes. Some people came to the doctor's office to be treated. Much of the time, however, the doctor had to travel to patients' homes, which might be many miles away. If a patient needed an operation, the doctor usually performed it in the patient's home—most often on the kitchen table.

In this photograph, taken about 1904, Dr. Mayo
stands beside the horse-drawn buggy he used
to travel to his patients' homes.

he was doing and why. Soon the boys were helping their father care for people who were sick or in pain.

Charlie and Will enjoyed working with their father. They both wanted to become doctors. On September 16, 1880, Will Mayo enrolled in the University of Michigan's medical school. He was nineteen years old. Three years later, in June 1883, he received his doctor's diploma.

Dr. Will's medical school graduation photograph, taken in 1883

During the early 1800s, it was not difficult to become a doctor. Many medical schools were run by just one doctor. Anyone could go to these schools, but most medical students were men. The students listened to lectures. They spent time helping and watching another doctor. After only about two years, students graduated and began to treat patients.

This 1892 photograph shows a classroom lecture in which
medical students (including a few women) watch
a doctor demonstrate surgical procedures.

Medical School Today

Today, students—both men and women—in medical school have already attended college for three to four years. Medical school lasts for another four years. After medical school, students train at a hospital. This training lasts from three to seven years. After the training is completed, a doctor can finally receive a license to practice medicine. (In the United States, it is illegal to practice medicine without one.)

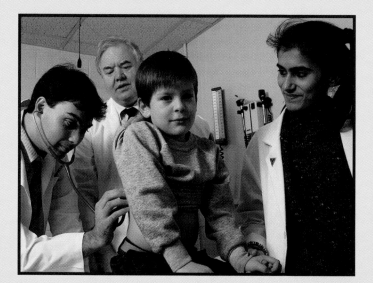

As medical students (left/right) examine a young patient, the students' teacher (in back) looks on.

But in the late 1800s, medical schools began to improve the way doctors were trained. Students had to pass certain requirements to be admitted to medical school. By the time Will Mayo attended the University of Michigan, medical training was much tougher.

After Will graduated from the University of Michigan, he returned to Rochester to help his father. Now there were two Doctor Mayos. Dr. Will, as he was called, continued to study medicine. His father had been very successful with stomach surgery. As a result, other doctors would travel to Rochester to watch him operate on patients. On Sunday mornings, he gave lectures to teach the doctors, including Will, what he knew about practicing medicine and performing surgery.

Dr. Will and his father would also travel to watch other doctors. They wanted to keep learning different ways to become better doctors. Will's father believed that people must teach, help, and care for each other. In the summer of 1883, the Mayos would find out just how true that was.

Throughout his life, Dr. Mayo (center) encouraged
his sons Charlie (left) and Will (right)
to work continuously to learn new things.

A Hospital
for Rochester

August 21, 1883, was a hot day in Rochester. Dark clouds gathered in the sky. They began to swirl and quickly formed a tornado. The tornado tore through the town, ripping up trees and tearing down buildings.

The Mayos were not hurt, but hundreds of people in Rochester were not so lucky. All the doctors in Rochester came together to help the injured. Dr. Will and his brother Charlie treated the people who came to the Mayos' office. Their father performed surgery in a hotel because the town had no hospital.

Rochester, Minnesota, after the tornado
of August 21, 1883

The next day, a large dance hall in the middle of
town was turned into a hospital. Dr. Mayo knew he
would need nurses. He asked the Sisters of St. Francis,
a group of teaching nuns, to help. (A nun is a woman,
known as a sister, who lives in a religious community

Mother Alfred (pictured here about 1883) believed a hospital should be built in Rochester.

and has promised to devote her life to God.) Mother Alfred, the head of the Sisters of St. Francis, sent sisters to help for as long as they were needed.

This disaster gave Mother Alfred an idea. She wanted to build a hospital for Rochester. She told Dr. Mayo about her idea. The doctor believed that after the emergency was over, there wouldn't be enough patients to fill a hospital. But Mother Alfred knew that the city needed a hospital. After raising enough money to build the hospital, Mother Alfred again asked Dr. Mayo to help. He agreed.

22

Charlie Mayo had not yet finished public school when Mother Alfred decided that Rochester should have a hospital. It took some time to raise the money and to build the hospital. By the time St. Marys Hospital was opened, in 1889, Charlie had become a doctor.

This photo of St. Marys Hospital was taken shortly after it opened in 1889.

The 1888 graduating class of Chicago Medical College

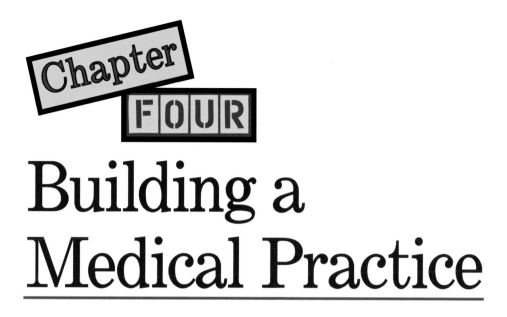

Building a
Medical Practice

Charlie had entered Chicago Medical College in 1885. His medical training was different from Will's. The Mayos considered this a good thing. They believed it would bring new information and better techniques to their medical practice in Rochester.

While in school, Charlie learned about a new way to do surgery. It was known as Listerism. Will had learned about it, too. They decided to use Listerism in all of the surgery performed at St. Marys Hospital. In September 1889, Dr. Charlie used it there for the first time.

Listerism

Joseph Lister was a British surgeon who learned that small organisms called bacteria cause plants and animals to decay, or rot. Decay in a human body becomes an infection. It used to be common for people who had surgery to die soon after. Most of them died from infec-

Joseph Lister
(1827–1912)

tion that occurred following their surgery. Dr. Lister found that the key to avoiding infection was to keep everything clean—including the doctor's hands, the instruments, and the area around the patient.

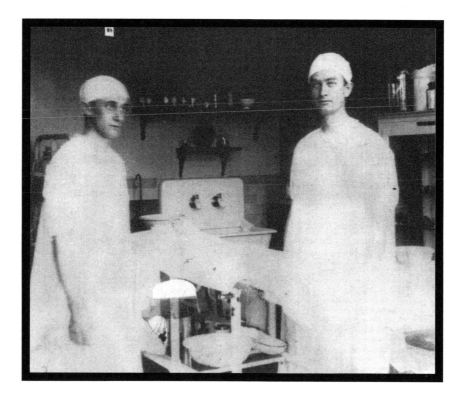

**Dr. Charlie (left) and Dr. Will (right)
in surgical gowns in the operating room
of St. Marys Hospital, about 1904**

Dr. Charlie and Dr. Will kept everything in St. Marys operating room clean. They wore rubber gloves and clean, white surgery gowns when they operated. The Mayo brothers already were good surgeons. When they began to use Listerism, they became even better.

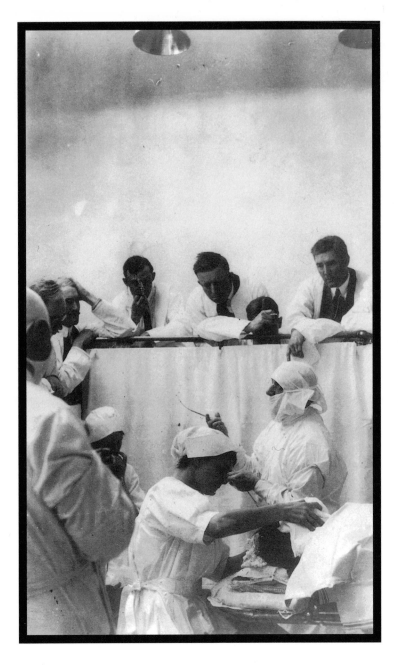

Doctors visited the Mayos to observe them at work. Here, Dr. Charlie (in mask, holding surgical instrument) operates on a patient while discussing the case with visitors. This photograph was taken sometime between 1913 and 1922.

Word about the Mayo brothers' skill in surgery began to spread. Patients from outside Rochester started to come to the Mayos for help. Other doctors began to send their patients to the Mayos for operations.

Many doctors could not believe what they heard about the Mayo brothers' success. In response, Dr. Will said, "Come see." A lot of doctors did just that. The brothers were always glad to share what they had learned.

Dr. Will and Dr. Charlie did not depend on their early success. They continued to learn and to study. They always were looking for new ways to be better doctors. Both men kept in mind what their father had taught them: People should teach, help, and care for each other.

As their skills improved, their reputations grew. Soon, people from other states began to seek the Mayo brothers' help. Between teaching other doctors and treating patients, Dr. Will and Dr. Charlie were kept very busy.

Chapter FIVE

Mayo Clinic

By 1892, the Mayo brothers were so busy, they knew they needed help. Their father was now a Minnesota state senator. He left Dr. Will and Dr. Charlie in charge of the hospital. They also ran the Mayo medical practice. The brothers began to invite other doctors to join them.

These doctors became partners in the Mayo medical practice. Each new doctor had an area of medicine that he did best. One doctor was the best at examining patients and finding out the cause of their sickness. Another doctor worked best in a laboratory, a place with special equipment for doctors to use in scientific experiments. All of these doctors added new ideas and new ways of doing things.

30

The Mayo brothers with some fellow doctors (from left):
E. Starr Judd, Dr. Will, Sir Rickman Godlee,
Christopher Graham, Dr. Charlie, and Donald Balfour

As more doctors and patients came to Rochester,
St. Marys Hospital had to be expanded. The Mayos'
medical offices were moved to a larger space.

The Mayo brothers' success was good for Rochester, but the city was still small. The Mayo brothers decided to help their city. They set aside a portion of their income to provide Rochester with places for recreation, education, music, and the arts.

Rochester's main street, about 1905

Dr. Will and his wife Hattie

In 1904, the brothers' first gift to the city was a public park. By this time, both brothers had married, and their families enjoyed picnics. Dr. Will had married Hattie Damon in 1884. They had two daughters. In 1893, Dr. Charlie had married Edith Graham. Edith was a nurse who worked in the Mayos' medical practice. By the time the park was

Dr. Charlie's wife Edith, with four of their children, in 1904 (from left): Charles Jr., Edith (seated), Joe, and Dorothy

built, Dr. Charlie and Edith had four children. (Eventually, their family would include six children.)

The Mayos' offices also needed more space. In 1914, the brothers moved their medical practice into a newly constructed building. When it opened, it became known as Mayo Clinic.

Mayo Clinic

Mayo Clinic was the first one of its kind. All the doctors in the clinic worked together. Any patient going through the clinic was examined from head to toe. In the process, the patient would be seen by many doctors. Afterward, the doctors would meet to decide on the best treatment for the patient. Before Mayo Clinic, other doctors might share offices, but each doctor treated his own patients.

The original Mayo Clinic building, in 1914

Doctors to the World

The Mayo brothers were proud of Mayo Clinic. They were sad, however, that their father had not lived to see it. Dr. William Worrall Mayo had died in 1911, at the age of ninety-two—three years before it opened.

Like their father, the Mayo brothers were more interested in helping people than in making a lot of money. No patients were asked to pay more than they could afford. Sometimes poor patients were not charged at all. Most people, though, were able to afford treatment. This made Dr. Will and Dr.

Today, this monument to Dr. Will and Dr. Charlie, located in
Rochester's Mayo Park, commemorates their generosity.

Charlie wealthy. But great wealth made the brothers uncomfortable. Their parents had taught them that no one should have a lot of money when there were others who were poor.

The Mayo brothers began to look for new ways to use their money to help people. First, they set up a fund to take care of their families. Then, in 1914, they created a foundation. A foundation is a group of people who give money to places such as schools or hospitals. The Mayos' foundation gave money for a program of special medical studies. The students in the program trained at Mayo Clinic.

The brothers' reputation spread throughout the world. Doctors from Europe, Asia, and South America went to the clinic to learn. People went there from all over the United States and many countries. In the halls of Mayo Clinic, a teacher from Texas might meet a princess from Great Britain. So many people from Mexico went to the clinic that many staff members learned to speak Spanish.

As more patients arrived at the clinic, the building needed more space. In 1928, Mayo Clinic moved

Dr. Charlie, shown here with two of his sons, Joe (front) and Charles Jr. (back). The Mayo brothers took steps to be sure their families would have money for their future needs, especially the children's educations.

Mayo Today

Today, Mayo Clinic is called simply, "Mayo." It includes three clinics, three hospitals, and a health-care system. Also included are a retirement community and a medical school. The clinics are located in Minnesota, Florida, and Arizona. Two Mayo hospitals are located in Rochester. One of them is St. Marys. The third hospital is in Jacksonville, Florida. Mayo Health System helps people in Minnesota, Iowa, and Wisconsin.

Today, St. Marys Hospital still operates in Rochester.

into another building that was twice the size of the old one. That same year, Dr. Will, at age sixty-seven, decided it was time to stop performing surgery. Eighteen months later, Dr. Charlie stopped, too. Both doctors continued to see patients in the clinic. They also advised the other doctors.

In 1932, Dr. Will and Dr. Charlie ended much of their work at the clinic. They spent time with their families, traveled, and enjoyed their hobbies. One of Dr. Will's hobbies was watching the stars and planets, which he had learned as a boy from his mother. Dr. Charlie liked farming.

The Mayo brothers received many honors and awards for their work in medicine. They were also honored for their many gifts to their community of Rochester, Minnesota.

In May 1939, Dr. Charlie died at the age of seventy-three. Two months later, Dr. Will died. He was seventy-seven years old. People all over the world were saddened by their deaths. Dr. Will and Dr. Charlie were good surgeons, but that was not their greatest work. Inspiring other doctors was what

This plaque was awarded to the Mayo brothers by U.S. president Franklin D. Roosevelt in 1934 "For distinguished services to . . . humanity."

they did best. They encouraged doctors to keep learning, and to pass on what they learned to others.

Guided by their father's teachings, the Mayo brothers built a medical practice that continues their work today. Mayo Clinic provides medical service, information, and education to the community of Rochester and to the world.

In this 1939 photograph, hundreds of people stand in
line at Dr. Charlie's funeral to pay their final respects.

In Your Community

The Mayo brothers shared their knowledge of medicine, and their money, with the community around them and throughout the world. You can learn more about the Mayo brothers' work and generosity by asking your community or school librarian to help you find other books and materials about them. The "To Find Out More"

Timeline

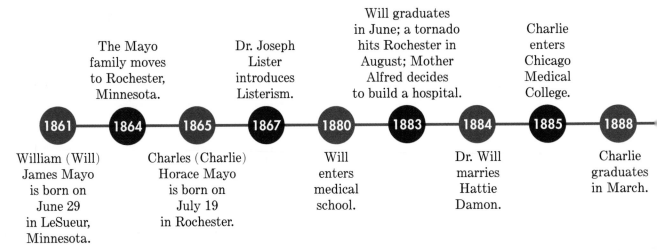

The Mayo family moves to Rochester, Minnesota.

Dr. Joseph Lister introduces Listerism.

Will graduates in June; a tornado hits Rochester in August; Mother Alfred decides to build a hospital.

Charlie enters Chicago Medical College.

1861 — **1864** — **1865** — **1867** — **1880** — **1883** — **1884** — **1885** — **1888**

William (Will) James Mayo is born on June 29 in LeSueur, Minnesota.

Charles (Charlie) Horace Mayo is born on July 19 in Rochester.

Will enters medical school.

Dr. Will marries Hattie Damon.

Charlie graduates in March.

section of this book is a good place to start looking.

Would you like to watch doctors at work? Ask an adult to arrange for you to take a tour of your local hospital or medical clinic. Perhaps you can give a report about your experience to your class.

Do you want to help people who can't afford medical treatment? Start by saving spare change. Perhaps your friends and their families would like to help, too. Donate your collection to a nearby hospital or medical clinic.

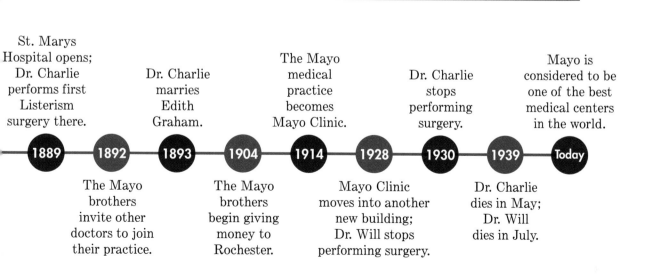

St. Marys Hospital opens; Dr. Charlie performs first Listerism surgery there.

Dr. Charlie marries Edith Graham.

The Mayo medical practice becomes Mayo Clinic.

Dr. Charlie stops performing surgery.

Mayo is considered to be one of the best medical centers in the world.

1889 **1892** **1893** **1904** **1914** **1928** **1930** **1939** **Today**

The Mayo brothers invite other doctors to join their practice.

The Mayo brothers begin giving money to Rochester.

Mayo Clinic moves into another new building; Dr. Will stops performing surgery.

Dr. Charlie dies in May; Dr. Will dies in July.

To Find Out More

Here are some additional resources to help you learn more about the Mayo Brothers, Mayo Clinic, and medicine:

Books

Bial, Raymond. *Frontier Home.* Houghton Mifflin Co., 1993.

Crofford, Emily. *Frontier Surgeons: A Story about the Mayo Brothers.* Carolrhoda Books, 1991.

Fradin, Dennis Brindell. *Minnesota.* Children's Press, 1994.

LeMaster, Leslie J. *Bacteria and Viruses.* Children's Press, 1985.

Organizations and Online Sites

Mayo Clinic Rochester
200 First Street S.W.
Rochester, MN 55905
http://www.mayo.edu/
General information about Mayo Clinic, Mayo's medical services, its history, and links to other sites.

Rochester Area Chamber of Commerce
220 S. Broadway
Rochester, MN 55904
http://www.hps.com/ Rochester/Welcome.html
The home page for the city of Rochester. You'll find information about schools, libraries, the city's history, photographs, and more.

American Medical Association (AMA)
http://www.ama-assn.org
Information about science and general health, including a site called KidsHealth.

Index

About
the Author

Lucile Davis is a native Texan, living in Fort Worth. She is a writer and a publications designer. She volunteers her time to help the Fort Worth Public Library. Interested in helping other writers, she also coordinates a writers' network in her area.

A number of Ms. Davis's relatives have gone to Mayo Clinic for help. All of them were pleased with the treatment they received. This made learning about the Mayo brothers very interesting.